COOKING THE CHINESE WAY

This book is available in two editions:
Library binding by Lerner Publications Company,
    a division of Lerner Publishing Group
Soft cover by First Avenue Editions,
    an imprint of Lerner Publishing Group
241 First Avenue North
Minneapolis, MN 55401 U.S.A.

Website address: www.lernerbooks.com

Library of Congress Cataloging-in-Publication Data

Yu, Ling (Lorraine Ling)
    Cooking the Chinese way / by Ling Yu.—Rev. & expanded.
        p.   cm. — (Easy menu ethnic cookbooks)
    Includes index.
    ISBN: 0–8225–4104–1 (lib. bdg. : alk. paper)
    ISBN: 0–8225–4160–2 (pbk. : alk. paper)
    1. Cookery, Chinese—Juvenile literature. 2. Quick and easy cookery—
Juvenile literature. 3. Low-fat diet—Recipes—Juvenile literature.
4. Holidays—China—Juvenile literature. [1. Cookery, Chinese. 2. China—
Social life and customs. 3. Holiday cookery.] I. Title. II. Series.
TX724.5.C5 Y58 2002
641.5951—dc21   00–012934

Manufactured in the United States of America
1 2 3 4 5 6 – JR – 07 06 05 04 03 02

easy menu ethnic cookbooks

COOKING

revised and expanded

THE

to include new low-fat

CHINESE

and vegetarian recipes

WAY

Ling Yu

Lerner Publications Company • Minneapolis

Contents

Introduction

Despite the fact that people in many countries enjoy eating Chinese food, preparing Chinese meals at home is still unfamiliar to many cooks. Actually, there is nothing mysterious about basic Chinese cooking. It is economical and nutritious, as well as tasty. Chinese cooks choose the freshest vegetables, seafood, and meat and make careful use of flavorful spices and seasonings to create delicious, satisfying dishes out of relatively simple ingredients.

One way to understand Chinese food is to learn about the background of China and its people. Like every cuisine, Chinese cooking has been shaped by the geography, history, and culture of its native country. Knowing a little bit about these factors will help you to appreciate China's tasty tradition of good food, and you can begin cooking the Chinese way yourself.

Rice is essential to Chinese culture and cuisine. (A basic recipe is on page 32.)

RUSSIA

KAZAKHSTAN

MONGOLIA

KYRGYZSTAN

NORTH
KOREA

TAJIKISTAN

SOUTH
KOREA

Beijing ★

CHINA

Yellow Sea

Nanjing   Shanghai

Chengdu

Yangtze River

East
China
Sea

NEPAL

BHUTAN

TAIWAN

INDIA

Guangzhou (Canton)

INDIA

MYANMAR

VIETNAM

BANGLADESH

LAOS

HAINAN

South
China
Sea

PHILIPPINES

THAILAND

The Land

China is the oldest existing civilization in the world. Its sophisticated art, literature, philosophy, religion, and cuisine have developed over thousands of years. Basic to the character of the Chinese people is their relationship to the land. Farming has always been their chief occupation. Archaeologists have uncovered farming tools and pots containing grains of rice that date back to 5000 B.C. Such finds indicate that agriculture was an important part of ancient Chinese society, just as it is important to modern China.

China's farmers, however, have not always been prosperous. This is partly due to the size of the nation's population. One-fifth of all the people in the world live in China. China is not much larger than the United States in area, yet it has a population of more than one billion—over four times that of the United States.

In this vast country, less than fifteen percent of the land is cultivated, because of a sometimes severe climate and terrain that ranges from mountains to rocky plains. Thus, food has been scarce throughout China's history. With such a large population to feed and so little farming and grazing land, the Chinese seldom waste anything. Since many workers are needed to tend the land, Chinese farm families have traditionally been large and close-knit.

Stretching the food budget without sacrificing nutrition and enjoyment is a daily challenge. Meat is cut into small pieces. Vegetables are added to increase the size of servings. Rice or noodles are a basic part of every meal and are an inexpensive way to provide a filling meal.

Cooking Techniques

Through the centuries, Chinese cooking has also been adapted to an ever-present shortage of fuel. Because wood and other fuels for cooking have always been scarce, the Chinese have learned to spend a maximum amount of time on food preparation and a minimum amount of time on actual cooking.

Most ingredients are diced, sliced, or shredded because small pieces cook more quickly than large pieces. The seasonings are measured out ahead of time. Most cooking is done in one pot and usually takes only a few minutes.

One quick-cooking technique is the stir-fry method in which meats, fish, or vegetables are cut into small pieces and tossed rapidly in hot oil. This method was developed to insure that the nutritional value, flavor, and color of foods were not lost during cooking.

This young girl has no trouble eating her food with chopsticks, as they are common utensils in China.

Steaming food is another quick method of cooking that preserves flavor and food value.

Eating with Chopsticks

To many diners who are used to eating with silverware, chopsticks seem like tricky utensils at first. But chopsticks are not difficult to manage once you have learned the basic technique. The key to using them is to hold the inside stick still while moving the outside stick back and forth. The pair then acts as pincers to pick up pieces of food.

Hold the thicker end of the first chopstick in the crook of your thumb, resting the lower part lightly against the inside of your ring finger. Then put the second (outer) chopstick between the tips of your index and middle fingers and hold it with your thumb, much as you would hold a pencil. Now you can make the outer chopstick move by bending your index and middle fingers toward the inside chopstick. The tips of the two sticks should come together like pincers when you bend your fingers. Once you get a feel for the technique, just keep practicing. Soon you'll be an expert!

Regions of China

Historically, Chinese cooks have had to use every available food source. So they have learned to cook a wide variety of foods, such as unusual types of vegetables and seafood.

Often, the ingredients used in Chinese dishes reflect the regions from which the dishes come. Over the centuries, each area of China has developed its own distinct dialect, customs, and character. Because climate and available foods vary from region to region in this large country, each section also has its own unique kind of cooking. Although basic cooking techniques are the same all over China, each region features special ingredients and seasonings. In general, there are four main "schools" of Chinese cooking, each from a particular part of China.

Cantonese cooking is associated with the city of Guangzhou (Canton) and the surrounding region in southern China. Most of the Chinese who emigrated to other countries during the nineteenth century came from Canton, and for this reason, Cantonese food is the most familiar to people outside of China. For example, sweet and sour pork and wonton soup both come from Canton. Cantonese dishes are usually stir-fried and lightly seasoned.

The *Beijing* (*Peking*) or *Mandarin* style of cooking developed in northern China. Here, the staple food is not rice but wheat flour. The flour is made into noodles, steamed bread, and dumplings. The most famous delicacy of this region is Peking duck.

On the eastern coast, *Shanghai* cooking dominates. These dishes are strongly flavored with soy sauce and sugar and include a wide range of seafood, which is readily available in this seacoast region. On the whole, the food is rich and tangy because of the sauces used. Central China's Sichuan (Szechuan) region, whose capital city is Chengdu, produces a style of cooking characterized by hot, spicy dishes. This cuisine contains a great deal of hot pepper, garlic, onions, and leeks.

Most of the recipes in this book are simple and require few ingredients. Once you have learned the principles of Chinese cooking and have mastered a few basic recipes, you may go on to make more elaborate dishes or to create your own variations. Your efforts will have a delicious result—something good to eat!

Holidays and Festivals

Cooking styles may vary from region to region in China, but food and mealtimes are central to daily life in all parts of the country. In fact, rather than using a greeting such as "Hello," Chinese friends and family often ask each other, "Have you eaten yet?"

Food plays an even bigger role during holidays and festivals. Most families splurge on special delicacies for festive occasions, and many foods have symbolic meaning. For example, grocers and street vendors, even in the smallest towns, make sure to have plenty of oranges and tangerines on hand for the Chinese New Year. These bright symbols of sweetness and luck are a must-have for every household.

Many Chinese festivals have their origins in Buddhism, the main religion in China. However, most of these holidays are now observed by Chinese people of all beliefs. The dates of most traditional celebrations are determined by the lunar calendar, which has twelve months, each based on the cycle of the moon's revolution around the earth. An extra month is added every few years, similar to the practice of adding an extra day in a leap year.

The most important event of the year is Chun Jie, the Spring Festival. Also known as the Lunar New Year, this holiday takes place on the first day of the first lunar month (between late January and late February). The new year is about fresh starts and new beginnings, so it is very important to make sure that debts are paid, houses are clean, and pantries are well-stocked before the big day arrives. Many people buy new clothes, get their hair cut, and buy gifts such as flowers or food for friends and relatives. Each family must also be on good terms with the Kitchen God. According to Chinese belief, every family's stove or hearth is under the constant watch of the Kitchen God. In most homes, a small shrine above the stove holds a picture of the god and his wife. This guardian takes note of all of the family's actions, good and bad. Near the end of the last lunar month, the Kitchen God travels to heaven to report to the Jade Emperor, the ruler of all the gods. To send him on his way—and to convince him to speak well of them—the family prepares a good-bye feast. Typical foods served at this feast are cakes, sweet rice dishes, candied fruits, and even honey.

The proper decorations also have to be bought and put up around the house. During the days before the festival, many Chinese cities and towns hold street fairs where shoppers can buy traditional holiday decorations. Families fill their homes with flowers, plants, and even small flowering trees. On the day of New Year's Eve, a new picture of the Kitchen God is placed above the stove, since he will soon return from his journey. Each family pastes paper pictures of the "door gods" on the front door. These two mighty warriors protect the home from evil spirits and bad luck. Near the door hang red paper scrolls printed with short verses that ask for good luck and a prosperous new year. Bright red pillows, candles, lanterns, and even candy also appear in Chinese homes at this time of year. Red is an important color at all Chinese festivals, but it is especially popular during New Year's celebrations. Not only is it the color of luck and joy, but it also frightens away any evil spirits that might threaten this happy occasion.

On New Year's Eve, the real celebration begins. The family gather to pay their respects to heaven and earth, the gods of the household, and the family's ancestors. Offerings of incense, candles, tea, and food are made to these influential spirits with hopes for their favor and protection during the coming year. After these observances, everyone enjoys the reunion feast, a magnificent banquet of many courses. Close relatives try very hard to come home for this special meal so that the family can welcome the new year together. Chinese cooks prepare the luckiest foods and most exotic delicacies for this feast. Typical dishes include a whole fish or chicken, representing unity and prosperity, long noodles for long life, and coin-shaped clams and mussels for good fortune. Other special treats might be shark's fin, squid, and sea cucumber.

After the big meal, the family stays up late playing games, telling stories, and exchanging gifts. Children receive *lai see* or *hong bao*, small red packets of "lucky money." Firecrackers are set off near midnight, and in the early morning, the doors of the house are opened to let out the old year and welcome in the new. On New Year's Day, many people visit their local temples. They may also visit friends and relatives, wishing them joy and prosperity and sharing lots of tasty things to eat. Common foods include *jiao zi* (boiled dumplings) and a sweet, sticky rice cake called *nian gao* that is only eaten at this time of year. Chinese families also prepare a special tray of treats for guests. This tray is filled with all kinds of lucky goodies, such as melon seeds, nuts, cookies, coconut, and candied fruits.

In modern China, New Year's festivities wind down after the second day of the first month. But in ancient times, the holiday wasn't truly over until Yuan Xiao Jie, or the Lantern Festival. Still a popular event, the festival lasts two or three days but peaks on the fifteenth of the first lunar month, the night of the new year's first full moon. When the festival began over one thousand years ago, it focused on the earth's renewed fertility and the return of warmth, light, and spring rains after the long winter. These days, it's a time to enjoy music and parades. In the evening, the streets are filled with people admiring displays of glowing lanterns outside homes, temples, and shops. These lanterns come in all shapes and sizes, from brightly colored paper spheres to dragons and birds. In northern China, where the weather is still cold, lanterns

A colorful dragon joins the procession in China's Lantern Festival. The dragon is an important symbol of luck in Chinese culture.

made of ice make a stunning sight. Everyone enjoys *yuan xiao*, the sweet rice flour dumplings that are the traditional food of the Lantern Festival. Eaten alone or in a broth, these treats are filled with tasty surprises such as dates, nuts, sesame seeds, or spiced meat. Their roundness is symbolic of the first full moon of the year and of family unity.

Throughout the festival, many small parades feature musicians, stilt-walkers, and other performers. But the big events are the lion dance and the dragon parade. The lion struts to the rhythm of gongs, cymbals, and drums. Two dancers control the movement of his head, eyes, mouth, body, and tail. The beast pounces and prances down the street, often playfully chasing a ball representing a pearl or a sun, and sometimes accepting gifts from shopkeepers hoping to receive good fortune in return.

The dragon parade usually takes place on the last day of the festival. Like the lion, the dragon's movements are controlled by people underneath its head or body. Many people are required for this creature, which may be more than one hundred feet long. The dragon is one of the luckiest and most powerful symbols in Chinese culture, and everyone turns out to see his majestic procession through the streets.

The biggest festival of the summer in China is Duan Wu Jie, the colorful Dragon Boat Festival. This celebration takes place on the fifth day of the fifth lunar month (usually sometime in June). The shores of lakes and rivers are crowded with people, as long slender boats carved and painted to look like dragons line up in the water to race. Most boats hold at least twenty rowers, plus musicians playing drums and gongs to keep them rowing in time. The Dragon Boat Festival probably began as a tribute to the river god, a dragon who controlled rivers and rain. But the celebration is also in memory of Qu Yuan, a famous Chinese poet and patriot who lived more than two thousand years ago. Zong zi (stuffed rice dumplings) are the traditional food of the Dragon Boat Festival. After the boat races are over, the festivities last into the night as people stroll though the streets, snacking on tasty zong zi and enjoying music and other performances.

Later in the summer, Gui Jie, or the Feast of the Hungry Ghosts, honors departed souls that don't have anyone to care for them. Chinese legend states that during the seventh lunar month the gates to the underworld are opened and spirits wander freely about the earth. Ghosts without descendants to feed them are hungry and may become unfriendly. To soothe their tempers, Chinese families offer these lost spirits food and gifts throughout the month. The offerings are made outdoors, since no one really wants the ghosts in their homes. On the fifteenth day of the month, many people visit Buddhist temples, where priests say prayers for the dead and toss them sweets (which are usually snatched up by the crowd). At the end of the month, the ghosts return to the underworld until the next year, full and content.

As summer ends and autumn's cooler days arrive, China's farmers harvest their crops of wheat and rice. On the fifteenth of the eighth lunar month (usually sometime in September), Zhong Qiu Jie, the Mid-Autumn Festival, celebrates this harvest. But the main focus of the festival is the moon, which appears fuller and brighter on this night than at any other time of the year.

Men perform most traditional and religious ceremonies in China. However, the moon is considered a feminine symbol, and women have always conducted the rites of the Mid-Autumn Festival. Candles and incense are lit on a special outdoor altar, and offerings are made of apples, melons, pomegranates, and peaches. These round fruits resemble the full moon and symbolize many children and long life. A clay statue of a rabbit may also sit on the altar, representing the moon hare who lives on the moon and mixes a potion of eternal life.

The most important offering of the night is the pyramid-shaped pile of thirteen moon cakes. These pastries may be filled with sweet bean paste, fruit, nuts, or heartier fillings such as vegetables or seasoned meat. They may be round or shaped like a rabbit, pagoda, or other figure, and they often have a design pressed into the top. Chinese bakeries display tempting stacks of moon cakes before the festival, but many cooks still make their own. Although not all Chinese families observe the traditional ceremony, most people still enjoy this festival and gather with friends and relatives to munch on moon cakes and to admire the full moon.

China also observes a number of national holidays. For example, most workers get two days off at the beginning of October to celebrate National Day. This holiday marks the anniversary of the founding of the People's Republic of China in 1949 and is usually celebrated with public fireworks displays and parties or parades. On June 1, Children's Day, Chinese children enjoy presents and parties in their honor. However, most of these holidays are political or government-related, and they don't involve the delicious traditional foods that make Chinese festivals such a delight to the taste buds.

Before You Begin

Chinese cooking makes use of some ingredients that you may not know. Sometimes special cookware is used, too, although the recipes in this book can easily be prepared with ordinary utensils and pans.

The most important thing you need to know before you start is how to be a careful cook. On the following page, you'll find a few rules that will make your cooking experience safe, fun, and easy. Next, take a look at the "dictionary" of utensils, terms, and special ingredients. You may also want to read the list of tips on preparing healthy, low-fat meals.

When you've picked out a recipe to try, read through it from beginning to end. Now you are ready to shop for ingredients and to organize the cookware you will need. Once you have assembled everything, you're ready to begin cooking. Keep in mind that one special feature of Chinese cuisine is stir-frying. This cooking technique is very efficient, but it's important to prepare all of your ingredients before you actually start stir-frying. Measure out the spices and herbs, wash any fresh vegetables, and do all of the cutting and chopping called for in the recipe *before* you heat up the oil. Then, once the oil is hot, you'll be able to add each ingredient quickly and easily.

Vegetable dishes such as bean sprouts with scallions make use of China's native ingredients. (Recipe on page 53.)

The Careful Cook

Whenever you cook, there are certain safety rules you must always keep in mind. Even experienced cooks follow these rules when they are in the kitchen.

- Always wash your hands before handling food. Thoroughly wash all raw vegetables and fruits to remove dirt, chemicals, and insecticides. Wash uncooked poultry, fish, and meat under cold water.
- Use a cutting board when cutting up vegetables and fruits. Don't cut them up in your hand! And be sure to cut in a direction *away* from you and your fingers.
- Long hair or loose clothing can easily catch fire if brought near the burners of a stove. If you have long hair, tie it back before you start cooking.
- Turn all pot handles toward the back of the stove so that you will not catch your sleeves or jewelry on them. This is especially important when younger brothers and sisters are around. They could easily knock off a pot and get burned.
- Always use a pot holder to steady hot pots or to take pans out of the oven. Don't use a wet cloth on a hot pan because the steam it produces could burn you.
- Lift the lid of a steaming pot with the opening away from you so that you will not get burned.
- If you get burned, hold the burn under cold running water. Do not put grease or butter on it. Cold water helps to take the heat out, but grease or butter will only keep it in.
- If grease or cooking oil catches fire, throw baking soda or salt at the bottom of the flame to put it out. (Water will *not* put out a grease fire.) Call for help, and try to turn all the stove burners to "off."

Cooking Utensils

cleaver—A large, square-blade knife used to cut, slice, chop, shred, and section foods. A large all-purpose knife works just as well.

slotted spoon—A large spoon with holes or slots to allow liquid to drain

spatula—The curved Chinese spatula is used to toss, turn, and scoop up food, usually during stir-frying. Any kind of wooden or metal spatula can be used.

steamer—A cooking utensil used to cook food with steam. Most steamers have tight-fitting lids and racks or baskets to hold the food.

wok—The wok has been used in Chinese homes for centuries. It is an all-purpose pot with a rounded bottom and sloping sides that can be used for deep-frying, stir-frying, and steaming. A large skillet or an electric frying pan can be easily substituted for a wok.

Cooking Terms

boil—To heat a liquid over high heat until bubbles form and rise rapidly to the surface

brown—To cook food quickly in fat over high heat so that the surface turns an even brown

cut in—To combine a fat such as vegetable shortening with flour, by cutting or breaking the fat into small pieces and mixing it throughout the flour until mixture has a coarse, mealy consistency

deep-fry—To cook food by immersing it completely in very hot oil or fat. This cooking method seals in flavor and gives food a crispy surface.

marinate—To soak food in liquid to tenderize it and to add flavor

mince—To chop food into very small pieces

preheat—To allow an oven to warm up to a certain temperature before putting food in it roast—To cook in an open pan in an oven so that heat penetrates the food from all sides

simmer—To cook over low heat in liquid kept just below its boiling point. Bubbles may occasionally rise to the surface.

stir-fry—To cook food in a small amount of oil over high heat, stirring constantly. All the ingredients are cut into small pieces before stir-frying so that they cook rapidly. Because of quick cooking, meats are firm yet tender, and vegetables stay fresh and crunchy.

Special Ingredients

bamboo shoots—Tender, fleshy yellow sprouts from bamboo canes

bean sprouts—Sprouts from the mung bean. Be sure not to confuse bean sprouts with alfalfa sprouts, which are smaller and finer.

brown candy—A hard form of dark sugar available in packages or sometimes sold in bulk at specialty markets

chard—A vegetable with dark green, yellow, or bright red leaves. Its stalks and leaves can be cooked or eaten raw.

Chinese black vinegar—A dark vinegar with a deeper, smokier flavor than light rice vinegar. It is available at most supermarkets or specialty stores.

Chinese (celery) cabbage—A pale green vegetable with broad, tightly packed leaves, often used in soups and stir-fries. Other leafy green vegetables, such as fresh spinach or chard, can be substituted for Chinese cabbage.

cornstarch—A fine, white starch made from corn and used to thicken sauces. When using cornstarch, put the required amount of dry cornstarch in a cup and add just enough cold water to form a smooth, thin paste. Then add this mixture to the other ingredients. This method keeps the cornstarch from forming lumps when cooked.

duck or plum sauce—A thick sauce often used as a dip. Made from plums, chilies, sugar, and spices, it is available at most grocery stores.

garlic—A bulb-forming herb with a strong, distinctive flavor. Each bulb can be broken up into several small sections called cloves. Before you chop up a clove of garlic, remove the brittle, papery covering that surrounds it.

gelatin—A clear, powdered protein used as a thickening agent

ginger root—A knobby, light brown root used to flavor food. To use fresh ginger root, slice off the amount called for, peel off the skin with the side of a spoon, and grate the flesh. Freeze the rest of the root for future use. Do not substitute dried ground ginger for fresh ginger, as the taste is very different.

glutinous rice flour—A powder made from sweet or glutinous rice, available at most specialty stores. Also called sticky rice flour or sweet rice flour, this is different from regular rice flour and the two cannot be substituted for each other.

hoisin sauce—A dark, sweet, thick sauce made from soybeans, sugar, and spices. It can be used in cooking or as a dip. Hoisin sauce is available at most supermarkets.

oyster sauce—A sauce made from oysters, sugar, and soy sauce, used in cooking and as a dip. Oyster sauce is available at grocery stores or specialty markets.

rice—There are three main varieties of rice. *Long-grain rice,* the kind used in most Chinese recipes, is fluffy and absorbs more water than other types of rice. *Short-grain rice* has shorter, thicker grains that tend to stick together when cooked. *Sweet* or *glutinous rice* is used in Chinese pastries and special festival dishes.

scallion—A variety of green onion

sesame oil—A strongly flavored oil made from sesame seeds

soy sauce—A salty-tasting sauce made from soybeans

sugar (snow) peas—Tender, green pea pods

wonton skins—Small, thin squares of soft dough made from flour, water, and eggs. Dumpling wrappers are similar to wonton skins, but they are always round.

Healthy and Low-Fat Cooking Tips

Many modern cooks are concerned about preparing healthy, low-fat meals. Fortunately, there are simple ways to reduce the fat content of most dishes. Here are a few general tips for adapting the recipes in this book. Throughout the book, you'll also find specific suggestions for individual recipes—and don't worry, they'll still taste delicious!

Some recipes call for oil to sauté vegetables or other ingredients. Reducing the amount of oil you use is one quick way to reduce fat. You can also substitute a low-fat or nonfat cooking spray for oil. Sprinkling just a little bit of salt on vegetables brings out their natural juices, so less oil is needed. It's also a good idea to use a nonstick frying pan if you decide to use less oil than the recipe calls for.

Almost all Chinese cooking uses soy sauce, a seasoning that, like salt, adds a great deal of flavor but is high in sodium. To lower the sodium content of these dishes, you may simply reduce the amount of soy sauce you use. You can also substitute low-sodium soy sauce. Be aware that soy sauce labeled "light" is usually actually lighter in color than regular soy sauce, not lower in sodium.

Many Chinese dishes include meat or fish. However, it is easy to adapt most of the recipes in this book to be vegetarian. Tofu (a soybean product) or mock duck (a wheat product) make simple and satisfying substitutions for meat. Or try adding extra vegetables, especially hearty vegetables like mushrooms, sweet potatoes, or eggplant.

There are many ways to prepare meals that are good for you and still taste great. As you become a more experienced cook, try experimenting with recipes and substitutions to find the methods that work best for you.

METRIC CONVERSIONS

Cooks in the United States measure both liquid and solid ingredients using standard containers based on the 8-ounce cup and the tablespoon. These measurements are based on volume, while the metric system of measurement is based on both weight (for solids) and volume (for liquids). To convert from U.S. fluid tablespoons, ounces, quarts, and so forth to metric liters is a straightforward conversion, using the chart below. However, since solids have different weights—one cup of rice does not weigh the same as one cup of grated cheese, for example—many cooks who use the metric system have kitchen scales to weigh different ingredients. The chart below will give you a good starting point for basic conversions to the metric system.

MASS (weight)

1 ounce (oz.)	=	28.0 grams (g)
8 ounces	=	227.0 grams
1 pound (lb.) or 16 ounces	=	0.45 kilograms (kg)
2.2 pounds	=	1.0 kilogram

LIQUID VOLUME

1 teaspoon (tsp.)	=	5.0 milliliters (ml)
1 tablespoon (tbsp.)	=	15.0 milliliters
1 fluid ounce (oz.)	=	30.0 milliliters
1 cup (c.)	=	240 milliliters
1 pint (pt.)	=	480 milliliters
1 quart (qt.)	=	0.95 liters (l)
1 gallon (gal.)	=	3.80 liters

LENGTH

¼ inch (in.)	=	0.6 centimeters (cm)
½ inch	=	1.25 centimeters
1 inch	=	2.5 centimeters

TEMPERATURE

212°F	=	100°C (boiling point of water)
225°F	=	110°C
250°F	=	120°C
275°F	=	135°C
300°F	=	150°C
325°F	=	160°C
350°F	=	180°C
375°F	=	190°C
400°F	=	200°C

(To convert temperature in Fahrenheit to Celsius, subtract 32 and multiply by .56)

PAN SIZES

8-inch cake pan	= 20 x 4-centimeter cake pan
9-inch cake pan	= 23 x 3.5-centimeter cake pan
11 x 7-inch baking pan	= 28 x 18-centimeter baking pan
13 x 9-inch baking pan	= 32.5 x 23-centimeter baking pan
9 x 5-inch loaf pan	= 23 x 13-centimeter loaf pan
2-quart casserole	= 2-liter casserole

A Chinese Table

The Chinese way of serving food evolved on farms, where families were large and close-knit. Eating together with members of the family and with close friends was, and still is, a great pleasure in China. Chinese family meals are served in a communal style. The food is served on large platters and placed in the center of a table so that everyone can reach the dishes easily. Each diner takes what he or she wants from each platter and fills his or her own bowl.

Place settings are simple. To set a typical Chinese table, you need the following items for each person:

- *a pair of chopsticks*
- *a soup bowl*
- *a porcelain soup spoon*
- *a rice bowl and saucer*
- *a tiny saucer for bones*

With shared platters of food and simple place settings, unexpected guests at dinnertime can be easily accommodated. As the Chinese say, you need only add a bowl and a pair of chopsticks.

In a traditional Chinese meal, common plates of food are shared by many guests.

A Chinese Menu

In China, an informal family meal usually includes a light soup, a meat dish, a fish dish, and a vegetable dish. The foundation of the meal is rice or noodles of some kind. Fresh fruits instead of sweets are usually served for dessert. For a feast or dinner party, the menu may include twelve or more dishes, each of which is served as a separate course. A feast may begin with appetizers and then move through a succession of hot dishes and several soups. Rice or noodles and sometimes a sweet dessert are also included. Below are menu plans for one family meal and one dinner party, along with shopping lists of necessary ingredients to prepare each of these meals. The combinations of dishes below are only suggestions. It is fun to experiment and discover the menu plans that you like best.

FAMILY MEAL

Watercress soup

Stir-fried beef with sugar peas

Bean sprouts with scallions

Plain rice

Tea

Fruit

SHOPPING LIST

Produce

1 bunch watercress
2 c. sugar (snow) peas
5 scallions
1 lb. fresh bean sprouts or
   1 16-oz. can bean sprouts
½ c. mushrooms
fresh fruit

Dairy/Egg/Meat

1 lb. lean steak (any
   boneless cut)
¼ lb. lean pork

Canned/Bottled/Boxed

1 can beef or vegetable
   broth
1 can water chestnuts or
   bamboo shoots
soy sauce
oyster sauce
vegetable oil
sesame oil
cornstarch

Miscellaneous

long-grain white rice
loose Chinese tea
salt
sugar

DINNER PARTY

Wonton

Egg-flower soup

Spiced roast chicken

Shrimp with hoisin sauce

Pork with green pepper and pineapple

Chinese cabbage

Plain rice

Tea

Almond fruit float

SHOPPING LIST

Produce

4–5 scallions
several lettuce leaves
1 green pepper
2–3 carrots
1 lb. Chinese cabbage
1-inch piece of ginger root
1 garlic bulb
fresh fruit or 1 13-oz. can
   fruit with syrup

Dairy/Egg/Meat

½ lb. ground pork or beef
3- to 4-lb. chicken pieces
1 lb. medium-sized fresh
   shrimp or 2 7-oz. packages
   of frozen raw shrimp
1 lb. lean pork
2 eggs
milk

Canned/Bottled/Boxed

1 can water chestnuts
1 can chicken or vegetable
   broth
soy sauce
duck sauce
hoisin sauce
1 can pineapple chunks,
   unsweetened
almond extract
vegetable oil
sesame oil
cornstarch
1 envelope unflavored gelatin

Miscellaneous

1 package wonton skins
long-grain white rice
loose Chinese tea
salt
black pepper
sugar

* If you plan to do a lot of Chinese cooking, you may want to
stock up on some of the items on these shopping lists and keep
them on hand. Rice, tea, soy sauce, garlic, and ginger all keep
well and are common ingredients in many Chinese meals.

Chinese Basics

Rice is the basic food of the Chinese people. Most families eat rice two or three times a day, and Chinese cooks always have a large store of rice on hand. Rice noodles, rice flour, rice vinegar, and rice wine are all used in Chinese cooking. In fact, rice is so central to the cuisine that the Cantonese word for "rice," *fan*, is also used to mean "food." Before beginning a family meal, every diner traditionally invites each of his or her elders to *sik fan*, or "eat rice." This custom can take quite a while at a large gathering!

In addition to rice, tea has been an integral part of Chinese life for centuries. There are many kinds of Chinese tea, but the three main varieties are oolong, black, and green. Oolong, which is especially popular in China, is a pale brown tea with a distinctive flavor often compared to that of fresh peaches. Black teas have a stronger taste, while green teas have a fresh, light flavor. Jasmine-scented green tea has a delicate, flowerlike taste and aroma. Most tea is grown in southern and eastern China, and much of the harvest is still picked by hand. Selecting the best leaves and carefully preparing them is part of the Chinese appreciation for this much-loved beverage. Tea is drunk everywhere in China at all times of the day and evening, and no social gathering is complete without a pot of hot tea.

Tea is as common as rice in the Chinese diet. (Brewing instructions on page 33.)

Rice

This recipe is for plain, delicious white rice. Any leftovers can be used to make fried rice (see page 42), so you will seldom have to waste this versatile food.

2 c. long-grain white rice, uncooked

3 c. water

water for washing

1. Place rice in a pan or bowl and wash with cold water. Run your hands through rice and drain when water becomes cloudy. Repeat until water is clear.

2. Place rice and 3 c. water in a deep saucepan. Do not cover.

3. Put the pan over high heat and bring water to a boil.

4. Reduce heat to medium and cook for 10 minutes.

5. Cover pan tightly and simmer over low heat for 20 minutes, or until all water has been absorbed.

Cooking time: 40 minutes
Serves 4

* Congee, or jook, is a rice porridge that is commonly eaten for breakfast in China. Basic congee is very simple to make. In a deep saucepan, combine 1 c. short-grain rice and 8 c. cold water. Bring to a boil, cover, and reduce heat. Simmer for about 1½ hours, stirring every now and then to keep rice from sticking to the bottom of the pan. Just about anything can be added to congee, from veggies and meat to dried fruit and nuts. To quickly spice up this basic recipe, try topping it with chopped scallions and fresh, thinly sliced ginger.

Tea

Chinese tea usually comes in loose form rather than in tea bags. It is always drunk plain, without sugar, lemon, or milk. The following method of preparing tea will give the best results.

water

loose Chinese tea*

1. In a teakettle or saucepan, bring water to a boil.

2. Rinse a teapot (earthenware or china is better than metal) with a small amount of the boiling water.

3. Measure loose tea into the pot. One teaspoon of tea for each cup of water is a good rule of thumb, but the exact amount is really up to your own taste. You'll probably have to experiment a little to brew it just the way you like.

4. Pour boiling water into the teapot, cover, and let stand for a few minutes.

5. Pour tea into cups.

Preparation time: 15 minutes

* Tea isn't just delicious—it's good for you, too. Many people believe that drinking tea has a number of health benefits, including lowering cholesterol levels and preventing heart disease and cancer.

Appetizers and Soups

The Chinese name for appetizers is dim sum, which means "touch the heart." In China, these tidbits of food are usually served with tea as mid-morning, afternoon, or late-night snacks rather than before a meal. In Chinese teahouses, which are similar to cafés in other parts of the world, people enjoy gathering to share a pot of tea, a variety of delicious little treats, and long, relaxed conversations. Just a few typical samplings for dim sum are fried wonton, egg rolls, shrimp balls, filled dumplings, and sweet pastries.

While dim sum is a special treat, soup is an important part of almost all Chinese meals. Generally, a light, clear soup is served as a drink between courses or throughout a meal. In fact, soup is often the only beverage served with food. Many people choose to enjoy tea before or after, but not during, a meal.

At a formal dinner or banquet, several kinds of thicker, richer soups may be served as courses in themselves. In parts of China where the winters are cold, hearty soups and stews are a good way to warm up. Soup is usually served in a large bowl or tureen in the middle of the table rather than in individual bowls, so that diners can help themselves.

Egg-flower soup is a delicious meal on a cold day—or anytime! (Recipe on page 38.)

Wonton

The literal English translation of the word wonton is "swallowing a cloud." If prepared as a soup, the wonton do resemble white, puffy clouds floating across the sky!

½ lb. lean ground pork or beef

1 tbsp. finely chopped scallions

1 egg, beaten

1 tsp. salt

1 tbsp. soy sauce

1 tbsp. sugar

1 tsp. sesame oil (optional)

1 tbsp. water

65 wonton skins*

3 c. vegetable oil (for deep-frying) *or* 2½ 15-oz. cans (about 5 c.) chicken, vegetable, or other broth (for soup)

duck sauce (for fried wonton)

1. Mix all ingredients except wonton skins and vegetable oil or broth.

2. Put one tsp. of mixture in the center of a wonton skin. Moisten edges of skin with water and fold to form a tight triangle. Press edges together to seal.

3. Fill and fold rest of skins.

4. **For appetizers:** Heat oil in a large pot. Add a few wonton at a time and fry until golden brown and crispy, about 2 minutes per side. Carefully remove with a slotted spoon. (It is best to ask an experienced cook to help with the deep-frying.) Drain on a paper towel and serve hot with duck sauce.

5. **For soup:** Bring a large pot of water to a boil. Add a few wonton at a time. Do not overcrowd. Cook over medium heat for 8 to 10 minutes. Meanwhile, heat broth in a separate pan. Add cooked wonton to broth. Use about 3 dozen wonton to 5 c. of broth.

* Ready-made wonton skins can be found at many supermarkets. Since preparing 65 wonton takes a long time, you may decide to cut this recipe in half to make a smaller batch. If you save the extra wonton skins for later, you can keep them in the refrigerator for several days, or you can freeze them. Just be sure to thaw them thoroughly before using.

Preparation time: 1 hour
Cooking time for appetizers: 30 minutes
Cooking time for soup: 20 minutes
Makes 65 wonton

Egg-Flower Soup

This soup is easy to make and is a long-time favorite in China as well as in other countries.

½ c. chicken breast, cut into small pieces*

1 tbsp. cornstarch

1 c. water

1 c. chicken or vegetable broth

¼ c. thinly sliced water chestnuts

1 egg

1 tbsp. chopped scallions

1. In a small bowl, mix chicken pieces and cornstarch.

2. In a deep saucepan, combine water, chicken or vegetable broth, and water chestnuts. Bring to a boil.

3. Add chicken and cornstarch mixture and return to a boil for about 10 minutes.

4. Beat egg and stir slowly into soup.

5. Dish into a large bowl and sprinkle scallions on top.

Preparation time: 10 minutes
Cooking time: 25 minutes
Serves 4

*Try preparing this soup without the chicken and with ½ c. of sliced mushrooms to make a tasty meatless dish.

Watercress Soup

1 tbsp. soy sauce

1 tbsp. cornstarch

½ c. lean pork, cut into small pieces

1 c. beef or vegetable broth

1 c. water

1 bunch watercress, chopped*

1. In a bowl, mix soy sauce and cornstarch. Add pork. Let stand for 15 minutes.

2. In a deep saucepan, bring beef or vegetable broth and water to a boil.

3. Add pork and the soy sauce and cornstarch mixture. Cook over medium heat for 10 minutes.

4. Add watercress and cook uncovered for 2 minutes.

Preparation time: 15 minutes
Cooking time: 15 minutes
Serves 4

*As a variation on this recipe, try replacing the watercress with 2 c. of any chopped leafy green vegetable, such as Chinese cabbage, spinach, or chard.

Main Dishes

A Chinese meal usually consists of several dishes, each of equal importance to the menu. Many of these dishes are combinations of meat or fish and vegetables and thus can be well-balanced meals by themselves. But usually several dishes are eaten together, along with plenty of rice. Each of the recipes in this section feeds four people if served together with one or two other complementary dishes.

When you select a combination of entrées for your menu, consider the flavors and textures of each one. It is important for the different dishes to harmonize yet provide variety. For example, if you decide to include a sweet and sour dish with lots of crunchy vegetables, you might also want to serve a heartier dish such as a thick stew or fried rice.

The more you practice, the easier it will get to choose tasty combinations of dishes. In addition to your entrées, you'll find that it is also fun to select the perfect appetizers, soups, and desserts for a well-balanced menu.

Sweet and tangy, pork with green pepper and pineapple is typical of Cantonese cooking. (Recipe on page 48.)

Fried Rice

Making fried rice is an excellent way to use odds and ends from the refrigerator. Fried rice is very economical, and it can be a complete and nourishing meal by itself.*

4 c. cooked long-grain rice, cold
   (see page 32)

3 tbsp. vegetable oil

½ c. chopped onion

2 eggs, beaten (optional)

2 tbsp. soy sauce

1. Use a fork to loosen and separate grains of cooked rice.

2. Place a large skillet or wok over high heat. Add 2 tbsp. oil and heat thoroughly.

3. Fry onion to a light golden brown. Remove to a plate.

4. Add remaining 1 tbsp. oil to the skillet. Add eggs, if desired, and stir-fry until done.

5. Add rice to pan. Stir in soy sauce. Add onion, mix thoroughly, and continue heating until completely hot.

Preparation time: 10 to 15 minutes
Cooking time: 15 to 20 minutes
Serves 4

*To dress up your fried rice, try adding cooked vegetables such as green beans, sugar peas, chopped cabbage, mushrooms, or bamboo shoots. You may also use small pieces of leftover beef, chicken, or pork— or try tofu instead.

Fried rice is a delicious meal that is quick and easy to prepare.

Stir-Fried Beef with Sugar Peas

Remember to work quickly when you make any stir-fried dish. Have everything cut and measured before you start cooking. Cook the meat and vegetables just until they are tender.

1 lb. lean steak (any boneless cut)

1 tbsp. soy sauce

1 tbsp. oyster sauce (optional)

2 tbsp. cornstarch

1 tsp. sesame oil (optional)

1 tsp. sugar

2 c. sugar (snow) peas*

4 tbsp. vegetable oil

½ tsp. salt

½ c. sliced water chestnuts or bamboo shoots

½ c. sliced mushrooms

* If you have trouble finding sugar (snow) peas, use broccoli, green beans, or any other chopped green vegetable. Pork, chicken, or tofu may also be substituted for beef.

1. Cut beef across the grain into thin slices. (Meat is easier to cut thinly when it is partly frozen.)

2. Marinate beef in mixture of soy sauce, oyster sauce, cornstarch, sesame oil, and sugar. Set aside.

3. Remove stems and strings from sugar peas, leaving pods intact. Rinse and pat dry with paper towels.

4. Put 2 tbsp. vegetable oil in a hot skillet or wok. Add salt, sugar peas, water chestnuts or bamboo shoots, and mushrooms. Cook, stirring constantly, until peas become a dark green (about 2 minutes). Remove to a bowl.

5. In the same skillet, add remaining 2 tbsp. vegetable oil. Add beef mixture and stir constantly until beef is almost done (about 5 minutes).

6. Return sugar peas, water chestnuts, and mushrooms to the skillet and mix well until heated through.

Preparation time: 15 to 20 minutes
Cooking time: 10 minutes
Serves 4

Spiced Roast Chicken

3- to 4-lb. chicken pieces (drum-
  sticks, wings, and thighs)*

¼ c. soy sauce

2 cloves garlic, crushed

1 tsp. black pepper

¼ c. sugar

2 tbsp. vegetable oil

several lettuce leaves

1. Rinse chicken in cool water and pat dry with paper towels.

2. Mix soy sauce, garlic, pepper, sugar, and oil in a bowl.

3. Thoroughly rub chicken pieces with this mixture. Save unused portion of mixture for later use.

4. Place chicken on a plate and let stand for 2 to 4 hours in the refrigerator.

5. Place chicken on a rack in a roasting pan and roast uncovered for 1½ hours at 350°F. Turn chicken and drizzle with remaining soy sauce mixture every half hour during roasting.

6. When chicken is done, remove from the oven. Arrange pieces on a bed of lettuce on a serving platter.

Preparation time: 10 minutes
Refrigeration time: 2 to 4 hours
Cooking time: 1½ hours
Serves 4

*After handling raw chicken or other poultry, always remember to thoroughly wash your hands, utensils, and preparation area with soapy hot water. Also, when checking chicken for doneness, it's a good idea to cut it open gently to make sure that the meat is white (not pink) all the way through.

Tired of the same old chicken recipes? Liven up dinnertime with spiced roast chicken.

Pork with Green Pepper and Pineapple

This is a simple version of a sweet and sour dish, a traditional recipe that has become a favorite in Chinese restaurants all over the world.

1 lb. lean pork*

2 tbsp. soy sauce

2 tbsp. cornstarch

1 tbsp. sugar

½ c. pineapple juice (drained from can of unsweetened pineapple chunks)

3–4 tbsp. vegetable oil

1 c. chopped green pepper

½ c. thinly sliced carrots

1 c. pineapple chunks

1. Slice pork thinly. (This is easiest when meat is partly frozen.)

2. Combine soy sauce and 1 tbsp. cornstarch in a bowl. Add pork to this mixture, stir, and set aside.

3. Mix remaining cornstarch with sugar and ½ c. pineapple juice. Set aside.

4. Heat 3 tbsp. of oil in a large skillet or wok.

5. Add pork to the skillet and stir-fry 4 to 7 minutes, or until white all the way through.

6. Add pineapple juice mixture to meat and blend thoroughly. Remove from skillet and set aside.

7. If necessary, add up to 2 tbsp. of additional oil to skillet. Stir-fry green pepper, carrots, and pineapple chunks for about 3 minutes. Blend thoroughly with pork and serve.

* This flavorful dish can easily be adapted to vegetarian tastes. Simply double the amount of green peppers, carrots, and pineapple in place of the pork and enjoy over steaming white rice! Red bell peppers also make a tasty addition to the mixture.

Preparation time: 15 to 20 minutes
Cooking time: 15 to 20 minutes
Serves 4

Shrimp with Hoisin Sauce

The sweetness of hoisin sauce and the spice of ginger and garlic make this dish a rich, tasty treat.

1 lb. medium-sized fresh shrimp, shelled and deveined, or 2 7-oz. packages frozen raw shrimp, thawed*

½ c. water

1 tbsp. cornstarch

2 tbsp. soy sauce

½ c. hoisin sauce

¼ c. vegetable oil

2 thin slices fresh ginger root, peeled and minced

1 clove garlic, crushed

3 scallions, cut into 1-inch pieces

1. Mix water, cornstarch, soy sauce, and hoisin sauce in a bowl. Set aside.

2. Heat oil in a skillet or wok.

3. Add ginger root and garlic.

4. Add shrimp and stir-fry until they turn pink (about 5 minutes).

5. Add scallions and stir-fry for 1 minute.

6. Add sauce mixture and cook for 2 minutes.

Preparation time: 15 minutes
Cooking time: 10 minutes
Serves 4

* If you use fresh shrimp for this recipe, you may be able to have it peeled and deveined at the grocery store. Otherwise, you can do it yourself. Hold the shrimp so that the underside is facing you. Starting at the head, use your fingers to peel off the shell from the head toward the tail. Then, using a sharp knife, carefully make a shallow cut all the way down the middle of the back. Hold the shrimp under cold running water to rinse out the dark vein.

Vegetables

Fresh vegetables are a very important part of Chinese cooking, and most meals include a variety of seasonal produce. Many supermarkets carry a selection of Chinese vegetables, including sugar (snow) peas, bean sprouts, and Chinese (celery) cabbage. Bok choy, a variety of cabbage that has crisp white stalks and dark green leaves, is a particular favorite in China. Delicious in stir-fries or alone, bok choy is rapidly growing in popularity outside of China as well.

Vegetables can be cooked by themselves or combined with other ingredients. In most cases, the cooking time for vegetables is short so that the original color is retained and the texture remains crisp. This cooking method also preserves important vitamins and nutrients in the vegetables. The simple vegetable dishes in this section can be served as light complements to heartier main dishes, providing a satisfying variety in your menu.

Crisp, healthy Chinese cabbage is a welcome addition to any meal. (Recipe on page 52.)

Chinese Cabbage

1 lb. Chinese cabbage*

½ c. canned chicken or vegetable broth

1 tbsp. cornstarch

2 tbsp. vegetable oil

1 tsp. salt

1. Wash cabbage and pat dry with paper towels. Slice in half and remove tough core with the tip of your knife. Then slice the cabbage into 1-inch pieces.

2. Mix chicken or vegetable broth and cornstarch. Set aside.

3. Heat oil in a skillet or wok.

4. Add Chinese cabbage and salt. Stir-fry for 4 minutes.

5. Add broth and cornstarch mixture. Mix all ingredients well and cook about 30 seconds or until broth is heated through.

Preparation time: 10 minutes
Cooking time: 5 to 10 minutes
Serves 4

* Try using bok choy, stalks and all, in place of Chinese cabbage in this versatile recipe. The stem pieces will take longer to cook than the leafy pieces, so add them a minute or two before the leaves. For extra zip, briefly stir-fry 2 thin slices of fresh ginger with the oil in Step 3.

Bean Sprouts with Scallions

Crunchy bean sprouts and zesty scallions make a delightful accent to any meal.

2 tbsp. vegetable oil

1 lb. fresh bean sprouts, or 1 16-oz. can bean sprouts, drained*

1 tsp. salt

4 chopped scallions

1. Heat oil in a skillet or wok.

2. Add bean sprouts. Stir-fry for 2 minutes. Add salt.

3. Stir in scallions and cook for 2 more minutes.

Preparation time: 5 minutes
Cooking time: 5 to 10 minutes
Serves 4

* If you use fresh bean sprouts for this recipe, be sure to choose sprouts that are firm and white. Many Chinese cooks like to trim off both ends of the sprouts, which may have a slightly bitter flavor.

Desserts

The Chinese eat very few desserts. Usually they end a meal with fresh, seasonal fruit, such as oranges, melons, or pears. Pastries and sweet dishes are made in China, but most of them are either enjoyed as dim sum or are special festival foods that are rarely served with the daily meal.

In the West, people often end a Chinese meal with fortune cookies. Like chop suey, however, these cookies are unknown in China. A recipe for fortune cookies has been included in this book because they are so much fun to make and eat. Just remember that the first two recipes in this section provide a more authentic choice of Chinese sweets.

Top off a traditional Chinese meal with an almond fruit float. Your taste buds will thank you! (Recipe on page 56.)

Almond Fruit Float

This light, cool dessert makes a refreshing treat on a hot day.

1 envelope unflavored gelatin

1 c. water

½ c. sugar

½ c. milk

1 tbsp. almond extract

1 13-oz. can fruit with syrup, or
  1–2 c. fresh fruit, cut into
  pieces*

1. In a saucepan, dissolve gelatin in water. Place over high heat and bring to a boil. Then reduce heat to low.

2. Add sugar and stir until thoroughly dissolved.

3. Stir in milk and almond extract. Mix well.

4. Pour into a deep, square pan and allow to cool to room temperature. Then put in refrigerator to chill.

5. When cool, cut into cubes and serve topped with fruit and syrup. If there is not enough syrup with the fruit, make a syrup by mixing 1 c. of water with 3 tbsp. sugar and ¼ tsp. almond extract and heating until sugar dissolves.

Cooking time: 15 to 20 minutes
Cooling time: 45 to 60 minutes
Serves 6

* Any kind of fruit, fresh or canned, may be used in this recipe. Mandarin oranges, sliced peaches, fruit cocktail, and pineapple all make delicious floats.

Almond Cookies

Serve these little cookies as an afternoon snack with a pot of tea. What a treat!

2½ c. all-purpose flour

I c. sugar

I tsp. baking soda

¼ tsp. salt

I c. vegetable shortening

2 eggs, beaten

I tbsp. almond extract

¼ c. blanched unsalted almonds

1. Mix dry ingredients in a bowl.

2. Cut shortening into dry ingredients with a fork or pastry cutter.

3. Add beaten eggs and almond extract. Stir with a spoon until well mixed.

4. Preheat the oven to 325°F.

5. Shape dough into balls the size of a large cherry.

6. Put on greased cookie sheets. Press an almond into the center of each cookie to slightly flatten.

7. Bake for 15 to 25 minutes, or until lightly browned.

Preparation time: 20 to 25 minutes
Baking time: 15 to 25 minutes
Makes about 4 dozen cookies

Fortune Cookies

1 c. margarine, softened

½ c. sugar

1 egg

2½ tsp. vanilla extract

3¼ c. flour

½ tsp. baking powder

1. Combine margarine, sugar, egg, and vanilla. Mix until smooth. Add flour and baking powder. Stir everything together to form a ball of dough.

2. Lightly flour a wooden board or flat surface. With a rolling pin, roll half of dough very thin. Use a circle-shaped cookie cutter or the top of a large glass (about 2½ inches wide) to cut out circles in dough. (Cut dough into other shapes, if you wish.)

3. Put a fortune in each circle, off to one side.* Fold the circle in half and then in half again. Pinch edges to seal.

4. Preheat the oven to 425°F.

5. Reroll leftover scraps of dough and make cookies from them. Then roll and make cookies from other half of dough.

6. Bake cookies for about 10 minutes or until they are lightly browned. Serve when cool.

Preparation time: 30 to 45 minutes
Baking time: 10 minutes
Makes 25 cookies

Part of the fun of making fortune cookies is creating your own personal fortunes for each one. These fortunes can be anything from predictions of the future to old sayings. Be creative!

Holiday and Festival Food

Celebrations in China involve all kinds of special foods, some of which have been traditional favorites for hundreds of years. The festivities just wouldn't be complete without them.

In modern times, many of these delicacies, especially pastries, are sold in stores and markets. However, many Chinese families still find room in their busy schedules to make festival foods at home. Although this is time consuming, it gives cooks more freedom to make sure that these important meals are prepared just the way they like them. It's also a fun way to celebrate and to carry on the customs that their ancestors observed.

The recipes in this section give you a chance to try some of these traditional foods yourself. Prepare them for special occasions, or anytime, to enjoy a wonderful taste of China's holidays and festivals.

Sweet, rich New Year's cake is a favorite holiday dessert in China. (Recipe on page 64.)

Boiled Dumplings

Dumplings:

3 c. finely chopped Chinese
   (celery) cabbage

I tsp. salt

I lb. lean ground pork*

I c. chopped leeks

I tbsp. minced ginger

I tsp. minced garlic

I tbsp. soy sauce

I tbsp. cornstarch

I package dumpling wrappers

water

Dipping Sauce:

¼ c. soy sauce

2 tbsp. Chinese black vinegar

* To make delicious vegetarian dumplings, replace the pork with an extra 2 c. of cabbage and 2 or 3 c. of mushrooms, cut into strips.

1. In a medium mixing bowl, toss cabbage with salt. Set aside. After 20 minutes, squeeze cabbage dry and place in a large mixing bowl.

2. Add pork, leeks, ginger, garlic, soy sauce, and cornstarch. Mix well.

3. Place a heaping tsp. of filling in the center of a dumpling wrapper. Dampen fingers with water and wet the inside edge of the wrapper. Fold to make a half-circle and press edges together to seal. Repeat with remaining filling.

4. For dipping sauce, mix soy sauce and black vinegar and set aside.

5. Bring a large half-full pot of water to a boil. Add 10 dumplings, or as many as will fit without crowding. When water returns to a boil, add ½ c. cold water. Return to a boil, add ½ c. cold water, and boil a third time. Carefully remove dumplings with a slotted spoon and drain. Repeat with remaining dumplings. Serve warm with dipping sauce.

Preparation time: 45 to 55 minutes
Cooking time: 35 to 55 minutes
Makes about 50 dumplings

Preparing dumplings can be a big job, but it's worth it. To make it more fun, invite friends or family to help. Chances are, they'll stick around to help you eat them, too.

New Year's Cake

Red dates, the color of happiness and celebration, add a festive touch to this traditional cake. Sometimes called jujubes, these dates can be found dried at most supermarkets or specialty stores.

4 to 5 Chinese dried red dates

cold water

11 oz. brown candy
   (about 5 slabs)

2 c. water, boiling

7 c. glutinous rice flour

vegetable oil

white sesame seeds to garnish
   (optional)

1. Soak dried dates in cold water until soft, about 30 minutes. Remove from water and cut into halves, removing the pits. Set aside.

2. Cut each slab of brown candy into two or three pieces and place in a glass or metal mixing bowl. Carefully add 2 c. boiling water and let candy dissolve and cool.

3. Place glutinous rice flour in a large bowl. Make a hollow in the center of the flour and pour the cool dissolved sugar (brown candy) into this hollow. Stir flour and sugar together.

4. When a dough begins to form, use your hands to knead it gently. If necessary, add cold water one tbsp. at a time until dough is smooth and shiny.

5. Lightly grease an 8-inch cake pan with vegetable oil. Place dough in pan and mold it to fill the pan.

6. Decorate the top of the cake with dates. Sprinkle sesame seeds over all, if desired.

7. Place pan in the rack of a steamer,* cover, and steam over high heat until cake begins to pull away from the sides of the pan, about 35 to 50 minutes. While steaming, check the water level. Add more if necessary.

8. Remove cake from steamer. Pour off any water that has collected on top of the cake. Set aside to cool. When completely cool, run a knife along the edge of the cake and turn it out of the pan. Wrap loosely in plastic wrap and refrigerate until ready to eat. (Cake is best if eaten the day after cooking.)

9. To serve, cut cake into small slices (not wedges). Serve at room temperature, or warm up by resteaming pieces on a plate.

Preparation time: 45 minutes
Steaming time: 45 to 60 minutes
Makes one 8-inch cake

---

* If you don't have a steamer, improvise by using common kitchen items. Place two glass mugs or a large tin can upside down in the bottom of a large pot with a tight-fitting lid. Fill with water up to about three-quarters of the height of the mugs or can. Carefully set a dinner plate on the mugs or can. The plate should not touch the inside of the pot. Place whatever is being steamed on the plate, place the lid on the pot, and bring water to a boil. As with a regular steamer, be sure to check the water level regularly and refill as necessary.

New Year's Noodles

In China, New Year's is something like a nationwide birthday party. During this festival, all Chinese people add a year to their age, no matter when they were born.

8 oz. dried rice noodles

12 dried Chinese or oyster mushrooms

1 c. chicken or vegetable broth

1 tbsp. soy sauce

1 tbsp. cornstarch

1 tsp. sugar

1 tbsp. peanut oil

1 tbsp. minced garlic

2 tsp. minced fresh ginger

1½ c. chopped Chinese (celery) cabbage

1½ c. bean sprouts

1 c. sliced bamboo shoots

1 tsp. sesame oil (optional)

1–2 scallions, chopped, for garnish

1. Prepare noodles according to package directions and set aside.

2. Soak mushrooms in warm water for 20 minutes. Squeeze dry, trim off stems, and cut into bite-sized pieces.

3. While mushrooms are soaking, make a sauce by mixing the chicken or vegetable broth, soy sauce, cornstarch, and sugar in a small bowl. Set aside.

4. In a skillet or wok, heat peanut oil. Add garlic and ginger and stir-fry until garlic barely begins to brown.

5. Add mushrooms, cabbage, bean sprouts, and bamboo shoots and stir-fry until tender (about 3 to 4 minutes).

6. Add sauce and noodles to pan. Lower heat, and simmer uncovered for 3 to 5 minutes.

7. Sprinkle with sesame oil, if desired, and toss well. Remove from heat, garnish with scallions, and serve.

Preparation time: 25 minutes
Cooking time: 15 minutes
Serves 4

Long noodles, a favorite dish at New Year's, are also served at birthdays to ensure long life.

Moon Cakes

These special pastries are more than just tasty treats—they also have a heroic history. According to popular legend, secret messages hidden in moon cakes helped Chinese revolutionaries overthrow their Mongolian rulers in the 1300s.

4 c. all-purpose flour

1 tbsp. baking powder

½ tsp. salt

3 eggs

¾ c. sugar

¾ c. unsalted butter or margarine, melted

2 tbsp. water

1½ c. sweet red bean paste*

1 egg or egg white, lightly beaten

1. Preheat oven to 375°F.

2. Combine flour, baking powder, and salt in a mixing bowl.

3. In a second bowl, beat 3 eggs and sugar until they thicken, about 10 minutes.

4. Add melted butter, water, and the flour mixture to eggs and sugar. Stir until the mixture becomes doughlike.

5. Using your hands, shape dough into a long rope about 1¼ inches thick. Cut into about 20 equal pieces.

6. Flatten each piece of dough into a circle about 3 inches across. Place about one teaspoonful of bean paste in the center of the circle and fold the edges of the dough toward the center. Pinch the edges together firmly to seal. (It may help to dampen your fingers with a little bit of water.)

7. Gently roll each cake into a ball and flatten slightly. Repeat with the remaining dough and filling.

8. Use a cookie cutter to lightly press a design into the top of each cake, or draw a design with a fork tine or toothpick. Place cakes one inch apart on an ungreased cookie sheet.

9. Lightly glaze the top of each cake with beaten egg. Place in the oven and bake for 30 minutes or until golden brown. Remove and allow to cool. Serve at room temperature.

Preparation time: 45 to 60 minutes
Cooking time: 30 minutes
Makes about 20 cakes

* Sweet red bean paste is sold in cans at most specialty grocery stores, but you can also make your own. Soak 1 c. of dried red beans (preferably the Tiensin variety, but adzuki will also work) in water for at least 3 hours. Drain and place in a saucepan with just enough water to cover the beans. Bring to a boil, drain, and rinse under cold water. Boil and drain again, then add fresh water and bring to a boil. Lower to a simmer and cook for 45 minutes to an hour, or until beans are very soft. Gradually stir in 1 c. sugar and a pinch of salt and remove from heat. Mash mixture in a food processor or with a potato masher until the biggest lumps are gone and leave to cool.

Index

About the Author

Ling Yu was born in Nanjing (Nanking), China. Before coming to the United States, she attended Providence College in Taiwan. Later she graduated from the University of Dayton (Ohio) with a major in home economics and a library science minor.

Beginning in 1970, Yu was the audiovisual librarian at the Reading Public Library in Reading, Pennsylvania. Prior to that, she worked at the library on the main campus of Pennsylvania State University. Yu has also been a freelance translator for publishers in Taiwan, specializing in the areas of child development and publishing. She has taught various courses and demonstrations in Chinese cooking, returning frequently to Taiwan to visit and to learn more about Chinese cuisine. Yu is retired and lives in California.

Photo Acknowledgments
The photographs in this book are reproduced courtesy of: Dean Conger/CORBIS, pp. 2–3; © Walter, Louiseann Pietrowicz/September 8th Stock, pp. 4 (both), 5 (both), 6, 18, 30, 34, 37, 40, 43, 44, 47, 50, 54, 59, 60, 63, 66; © Robert Fried Photography, p.10; © Nevada Wier, pp. 15, 26.

Cover photos: © Walter, Louiseann Pietrowicz/September 8th Stock, front top, front bottom, spine; Robert L. Wolfe, back.

The illustrations on pp. 7, 19, 27, 29, 31, 32, 33, 35, 38, 39, 41, 42, 45, 46, 48, 49, 51, 52, 53, 55, 56, 58, 61, 62, 65, and 69 and the map on p. 8 are by Tim Seeley.

Haddonfield Public Library
60 Haddon Avenue
Haddonfield, N.J. 08033